11 SIMPLE *Steps*

To Writing, Designing, Self-Publishing & Marketing Your Very First Book

JAIME VENDERA

CO-FOUNDER OF 711 PRESS

7-11 Press

I dedicate this book to my mother, Linda Fagan,
For always believing in me, supporting my crazy ideas,
Putting up with my screaming, & Driving me to be my best.

For information about this and other 711 Press titles and products, visit us on the World Wide Web at:
www.711press.com

Cover and Interior Design by *Scribe Freelance*
www.scribefreelance.com

ISBN: 978-1-936307-18-0

Published in the United States of America

In memory of
Joyce Foster
Who instilled in me
The love of writing

CONTENTS

INTRODUCTION

It is said that your first book is the hardest to write. I concur. I've been writing since I could hold a pencil but never pursued a writing career until 2000. At the turn of the century, I decided I could tap into my extensive vocal background and write a book on vocal methodology in about a month. That month turned into nearly four years.

What I discovered during those four years is that many writers can become plagued by lack of motivation, which can be a destroyer of many great book ideas. I hit many roadblocks during those periods, but it was my own fault. I was consumed with trying to figure out how to improve my writing skills, prepare my book for distribution, design my own cover, draw the illustrations (and I'm not an artist), and build a website, all by myself.

Trying to wear all those hats at once was exhausting. My solution appeared near the end of those four years—find professionals to complete the tasks I was unqualified to tackle so that I could focus on writing and the tasks I could do myself.

After releasing several books, I've fine-tuned that solution into eleven simple steps, eliminating the guesswork from writing, formatting, releasing, and promoting a book from beginning to end. This solution isn't anything new. In fact, there are multitudes of self-publishing books, but most are out of date the moment they hit the shelves because self-publishing rules are continually evolving and changing. Because of this fact, I've made *11 Simple Steps* special by creating an online companion resource with continually updated material at:

http://711press.com/11-simple-steps-links/

The online companion resource puts extras and links at your fingertips to help you bypass the roadblocks that can kill your book idea. Think of this resource as your *11 Simple Steps* workbook, a workbook that will continue to change and grow, following the changes in the publishing world.

Everyone has a book inside them waiting to be written. Don't lose sight of that book because of roadblocks thrown up by technical details. Use this book and the online resource companion to help you write and release your own book in minimal time.

Are you ready to get started? Great! Follow along with the steps in this book as you write your book, and you could be a published author within four to eight weeks. How do I know? I've done it! Before we begin, I want to mention that although *11 Simple Steps* is written from the nonfiction author perspective, the steps in this book will work for a fiction title as well. Now let's move on to Step One.

NOTE: All words and phrases that are **bold and underlined** refer to resources listed on:

http://711press.com/11-simple-steps-links/

STEP ONE
Choosing a Book Topic

B*efore you start writing*, you need something to write about. The secret to becoming a successful author is to write about what you know. **What are your interests/hobbies**? Do you like singing, fishing, quilting, designing computer programs, gardening, racing, chess, cooking, cleaning, boxing, or auto mechanics? Do you like horror, romance, satire, YA, or sci-fi adventures?

The first step is to choose a book topic, preferably one that interests you. I write books about vocal technique because I love singing and I understand the mechanics. I wouldn't write a book on ballroom dancing because I know nothing about dancing and it doesn't interest me.

Maybe you love bowling and you've mastered the 7-10 split. Sharing that secret would make a great-selling book! If you're a fiction writer and *Harry Potter* is your favorite read, you might consider YA (young adult) fantasy.

If a book topic eludes you, not to worry, book ideas are everywhere. You'll discover book ideas while driving, working, eating, sleeping, and even when playing. Start paying attention, and if a great book idea suddenly comes to mind, write it down. With the endless thoughts flowing through our minds every day, I guarantee someone else has picked up on the same idea as you—and you want your book out first!

My first book idea was to create a set of unique vocal exercises to isolate notes in my vocal range to increase vocal strength. This concept became the "Isolation Method," which has been used by thousands of singers. I reinvented ways to improve the age-old process of voice strengthening. It all started with that initial idea popping into my head, and if I hadn't followed through, someone else may have beaten me to the finish line.

Your goal is to finish first by picking a topic that interests you and then brainstorming ways to take that topic to the next level. An example of a great book is when a fishing enthusiast who has caught a ridiculous number of bass with a one-of-a-kind fishing lure shares his knowledge with others, showing them how to make their own lure. What fisherman wouldn't love great lure-making techniques guaranteed to increase his catch?

So, what's your amazing **book topic**? Write down your answer, and then add your initial thoughts in your **pre-writing notes**. Any ideas you have about your book, such as chapter titles, specific topics, etc., should immediately be added. Don't worry about typos for now; just write down your thoughts before you forget them.

RESEARCH, RESEARCH, RESEARCH

Now it's time for research. A great book must be up-to-date with the latest information. Go to your local library, search the Internet for articles, and buy books about relevant topics. When I begin writing a new book, I buy and research at least ten books in my related field. I list the titles in the **research book list**. I study each book, copying all important information into the **research notes** section.

These are my "study up" notes. They cannot be added to a book word for word. That would be plagiarism. You're studying other resources that contain up-to-date facts on your topic to build a framework or "skeleton" for your book.

Now that you're building that skeleton, here's where to find the "meat" for those bones. Go to online book sites, such as amazon.com, that feature book reviews. Reviews—both good and bad—are full of gold nuggets, because reviews tell you exactly what a reader loves and hates about a book. Reviewers will also tell you what information they feel was missing and what they'd like to see added to the book. The bits of information missing from other books are the **gold nuggets** that will turn your book into a treasure chest.

During the research stage, you'll become a pro note taker. I suggest keeping an audio recorder—hand-held or smart phone app—with you at all times. You can record voice notes on the go and transcribe them later. An audio recorder is a must because you never know who you'll meet. What if you bump into a celebrity or an expert in your field and they offer to be quoted in your book? Without an audio recorder, you might not remember what they said. It can happen! When I was writing the second edition of *Raise Your Voice,* many rock stars and professional vocal coaches offered quotes and articles.

Now that you've picked your topic and started the research phase, I suggest personally testing your research to make sure it's applicable. Continue taking notes as you do your testing. It will all become part of your book. On to Step Two.

STEP TWO
How to Write a Book in Seven Days!

Once you've completed your research, you CAN write a book in seven days. I wrote my *Mindset* book in three days. I'm giving you an extra four days to take the pressure off. How do you write a book in seven days? Let me start by telling you how "not" to write a book in seven days. I wrote *Raise Your Voice* by pen in a notebook. What a big mistake. It's a waste of time transcribing handwritten notes to a word processor! If you don't have a word processor, you need to get one. There are a variety of **word processing programs**. I use Microsoft Word.

If you've handwritten your book, you can refer to the **transcriber services** list to find people who will transcribe your handwritten notebooks and audio recordings for less than you'd think.

I once had ten hours of audio notes transcribed. Doing it myself would have taken a week! That's time better spent writing. If you don't mind wasting time transcribing yourself, have at it. Otherwise, hire a transcriber.

Another option is using **transcription software** for your computer or phone, which transcribes as you speak. I've used an iPhone transcription app for small amounts of notes and it worked fine, though editing was required to correct the many typos. Still, it was quicker than transcription by hand. Now that you have your initial notes on your computer, it's time for Day One:

DAY ONE: CHAPTER TITLES & RESEARCH NOTES

The most efficient way to organize your book is to think of it as a step-by-step instruction booklet. When you buy a piece of DIY furniture, such as a hutch for your entertainment system, you must follow the instructions in the exact order to build it. If you skip a step, something won't fit.

How-to books are step-by-step instructions, written in exact order, to help the reader produce a finished product. Even fiction books have a beginning, which sets up the story; a middle, to introduce conflict; and an ending, for resolution.

Create a folder on your computer named after your book topic, such as "fishing book." Reread your **research notes** from Step One and use those notes to create a list of ten bullet points, minimum, by asking yourself, "What are the main points, based on my research, that I should cover in my book?" Write down the bullet points in your **chapter headings list**. Reorganize your bullet points in precise order from the most basic concept to the most advanced. I'm sure you've guessed that these bullet points will become chapter titles.

For *Raise Your Voice*, I had bullet points such as "breathing," "water," "health," "vocal exercises," and "recording," which I arranged in a step-by-step order to teach someone to sing from the ground up. I then reworded the bullet points into catchy chapter titles. For example, I came up with the title "Learning to Breathe Again" for my "breathing" bullet point.

Now it's time to turn your bullet points into chapter titles. Have fun with this assignment. Play with words. When you're finished, review each title. Does each one make sense and lead to the next chapter, or do you need to reorganize your list to build from basic concepts to advanced ones? Once you're satisfied with the names and the order of your basic chapter titles, it's time to transfer your **research notes** to the appropriate chapter. For instance, I added my breathing research notes to my "Learning to Breathe Again" chapter.

Writing is a continual process, so you'll continue adding notes as you build your book. You might also think of new chapters to include, some that need to be removed, or even two chapters that should be combined into one. It's your book, so add or remove as many chapters as needed. Congrats, you've finished Day One. Get some sleep, tomorrow will be a doozie.

DAY TWO: ORGANIZING EACH CHAPTER

Now that the chapters and notes are organized, start at Chapter One and begin organizing your notes into a working order. Remember, each chapter is a step to complete a project. Your goal is to help your reader complete each step with ease, which means making each step flow. Most likely your notes will not be in a flowing order. You must rewrite and reorganize for continuity.

It's fairly easy to move your notes around by using the cut/paste commands in a word processor. Typically, you first highlight a block of text by holding the left click on the mouse and dragging to the end of the block. To cut the block, press control X. Place your cursor where you want the text to appear and press control V to paste it in place.

Once the notes seem to flow, it's time for rewrites. Remember, most of your notes were copied from other sources. If you do not rewrite in your own words, you're plagiarizing. This is illegal. Read through a section, absorb it, and then rewrite a section in a separate document. These are short, sweet writing bursts to make sure you have the heart of each section. When you're satisfied, delete the notes and replace with your own wording. You're not worried about writing a masterpiece at the moment, so write quick, simple lines in the same wording you'd use to explain it to a friend. Keep it simple and we'll add as we move along. Once you've finished the rewrites, grab dinner and go to bed.

DAY THREE: BUILDING BRIDGES

Now it's time to expand on your rewrites. When I was writing *Raise Your Voice*, I had several notes organized in my "Learning to Breathe Again" chapter. A few of these notes were:

1. Need to breathe correctly using the correct muscles.
2. Breath control leads to voice control.
3. Air is a singer's fuel.
4. Three different types of breathing.

It was the same when I produced the TV Book series, *Age of the Sigil* for 711 Press (www.711press.com). I knew:

1. There were four teenagers.
2. Each had tattoos that turned into magical weapons.
3. They had to fight an evil wizard to save their continent.
4. They had to travel the lands to unlock their powers in order to win the battle.

Your initial notes won't fill up a chapter, let alone a book. To beef up your book, you'll build bridges between your notes by writing sentences between each note section to tie them together. Here's what I came up with for *Raise Your Voice*:

> *You must learn to **breathe correctly**, in order to gain*

maximum breath control. **Maximum breath control leads to maximum voice control.** *Don't freak out and think that you must control your voice; this isn't the case. Singing should be a natural and relaxed act. What this basically means is that the way you breathe affects your singing voice.* **Air is your fuel**—*your source of energy. Air feeds the voice and provides the energy needed to sustain the song within you, but you must learn how to control the amount of fuel you use to feed your voice, because most singers are using much more fuel than is necessary. If you do not breathe properly, your vocal cords will not vibrate properly. I cannot put it any simpler. There are* **three types of breathing** *that I am going to explain. They are chest breathing, diaphragmatic breathing, and what I like to call your "maximum breath potential."*

You'll find that building bridges helps to get the creative juices flowing. If you still lack information, read more books and reviews. If you feel your writing is weak, there are tons of **writing guides** such as my favorite, *The 7 Points of Write* by Daniel Middleton. Don't let your writing skills slow you down. Keep writing as you study. You never want to lose an idea, no matter how sloppy it may look as you're writing it. You will edit and refine your work at the end.

If writing still eludes you, you can hire a *ghostwriter* from our **ghostwriter services** list. A ghostwriter is someone who writes the book for you, based on information you provide. Make sure to get a written contract that states that YOU are the owner and, for all intents and purposes, the "author" of the book. They write it, you pay them, the job is done.

Before ending this section, I want to point out that a book

is finished once you've summed up the purpose of the book. In other words, don't obsess over page count. I've written books with 20, 80, and 400 pages, all equally informative. Don't expand a book just because you feel you need to beef up the number of pages. I'm not suggesting you shouldn't elaborate, but only expand if necessary.

Before moving on, have you backed up your document? You'd better! Once, after an eight-hour day of writing *Raise Your Voice*, my computer crashed and I lost the entire day's work because I didn't back up my document. I now make it a habit to keep a flash drive on hand so that I have two copies of my work.

The All-Important Title

Now that you're deep into Day Three, it's time to solidify your book title. I didn't do this on Day One because you needed time to organize your notes and allow the title to gel. Maybe you've already thought of a title. I hope it's an eye-catcher, because it needs to stand out among other books. Since my first book's topic was to extend the vocal range, I dreamed up the title *"Raise Your Voice"* which is a play on words based on singing and vocal range.

Your title can also have a subtitle, as this book does—*11 Simple Steps* (main title) *to Writing, Designing, Self-Publishing & Marketing Your Very First Book* (subtitle). The subtitle lets readers know more about the book topic. I've discovered that numbers catch people's attention, which is why *11 Simple Steps* and *The 7 Points of Write* contain numbers.

Now it's time for you to think up your **book title**. Don't worry if that eye-catching title still eludes you. Over the course of writing your book, you can play around with words until you find that eye-catcher.

That wraps up my three-day secret to book writing. All you need to write your book at warp speed is:

1. Add chapter titles.
2. Add research notes.
3. Build bridges.

I promised four more days, so get some shuteye and I'll see you tomorrow.

DAYS FOUR–SEVEN: REFINING YOUR BOOK

Once you've finished Days One, Two, and Three, the initial "write-through" is finished, but you still have a lot of work to do. The front of your book must have a copyright page and credits page for listing contributing authors, illustrators, etc., and a table of contents. You may wish to add a dedication page, foreword, and introduction.

It's nice to add extras at the end of a book such as a glossary for definitions of book terms, appendices for listing suggested reading or products mentioned in the book, final notes, or a recap of the book. An index that lists major terms and where to find them in the book is a nice touch. However, it can be a hassle because it can be thrown out of whack every time you update your book, which may be frequently considering the ease of updating digital content on sites such as Amazon KDP.

An acknowledgements section at the very end of the book is always a nice touch. Thank all your friends, family, and team members who helped you along the way.

In lieu of explaining these book extras in detail, your next assignment before moving on is to browse through your ten research books to reference the beginning pages and ending pages of each book (known in publishing as "front matter" and "back matter"). Use them as references for adding your copyright and credits pages, table of contents, etc., and decide what else would benefit your book. You have four days to accomplish this. I suggest you also use that time to read and reread your book, adding to your writing as you go. By the end of Day Seven, your book may have doubled or tripled in size simply because fresh thoughts surfaced as you read your own book.

Before ending Step Two, I want to suggest a way to boost your book-selling power—**professional contributors**. Once you've finished the seven-day draft, reach out to someone in your field and ask if they'd be willing to contribute an article to your book or write the foreword.

I asked singer Sahaj Ticotin from the band RA if I could use the song *SKY* in *Raise Your Voice*. I handed him a printed version of my book before it was released, along with my contact info, and asked him to read it before deciding. We've since developed a strong relationship. He has even contributed articles to the second edition of my book and sent professional singers to me for voice lessons.

You might be asking, How am I going to get an authority to endorse my book? It's easier than you think. The best way to get a celebrity or authority involved in your book project is to write them a sincere email. A person won't endorse a book without knowing who you are and knowing your work. When contacting an authority, tell them why you respect their work, and ask them if they'd be interested in reviewing and contributing to your book. End the email with all of your contact information.

Add an innovative subject header, or your email may end up in their junk folder. My subject header is, "Glass-shattering vocal coach seeks endorsement for revolutionary new book on voice training." Yes, that's a little crazy and maybe a little cocky, but that phrase has actually worked.

Send your letter to as many contacts as you can find for the person, including personal email accounts; Twitter, Facebook, or LinkedIn accounts; and the email accounts of their webmaster, manager, agent, etc. If it isn't directly to the celebrity or authority, address the email to the contact, asking to please forward your "introduction" email. I have landed dozens of endorsements and contributor articles. You can do it, too! Now, it's time for some book editing.

STEP THREE
Book Editing

Book editing is time consuming, tedious, and nerve-racking, but it must be done. I suggest you personally read through the entire manuscript three times, self-editing as you go. Check for typos and continuity. New thoughts will arise as you edit, allowing you to expand the material, tighten the concepts, and correct grammatical errors. All authors reread, rethink, and revise. That's why there are second editions, third and fourth printings, etc.

Here are seven simple self-editing tips to make the process easier:

1.   **Read backwards.** When reading normally, the brain takes snapshots of individual words. The only letters in a word that matter to the brain are the first and last. "So, if I deicde to intentoinally missepll a few words," your brain will decode them. Reading right to left eliminates the snapshots by forcing you to digest each word individually.

2.   **Simplify.** Simplify your sentences. Use "their" in place of "his and her." Shorten "he stood up" to "he stood". Delete words like "simply" or "actually." Extra words are fine, but overall, say what needs saying by removing unnecessary words.

3.   **Don't overuse words.** You *truly* don't *truly* need to *truly* use the same word, like *truly* repeatedly. You *truly* don't! Avoid repeats!

4. **Use a Style Guide.** Add MLA or APA to your bookshelf. They are listed under **writing guides** in Step Two.

5. **Read your work aloud.** Reading your work aloud allows you to hear how it sounds. Does it make sense when spoken? If not, it's time to restructure.

6. **Read your work in print.** Print your book and read it with a highlighter in hand. You'll catch mistakes by using the highlighter to lead your eyes. Highlight all mistakes. Once you've finished the print book, edit your word document.

7. **Double-check all information.** Information is updated every day, including new breakthroughs in your field, new websites, etc. Always double-check your facts and any web addresses you intend to list in your book.

Editor Richard Dalglish (rich.dalglish@verizon.net), who edits for 711 Press, gave me five more editing and proofreading tips for an even dozen:

8. **Pay attention to front matter and back matter.** It's easy to skim (or even forget) a table of contents or copyright page, especially after poring over thousands of words of main text.

9. **Triple-check chapter titles and subtitles.** If a typo in the main text slips through, some readers won't even notice. A typo on a chapter title or displayed subhead will stick out.

10. **Use the active voice.** But don't be a fanatic about it. You wouldn't change "the shot heard around the

world" to "the shot that everyone around the world heard."

11. **Make sure subheads are consistent.** It's a good idea to keep a cheat sheet handy with the formatting for each level of subhead written on it.

12. **Strive for consistency of usage.** Is it "five dollars," "5 dollars," "$5," or "$5.00"? It's your choice, but be consistent. Again, use a simple, handwritten cheat sheet.

Editing is a great skill to master. For further information, refer to the **editing tips** section. Once you're confident about your own editing, pass your document off to a professional editor. An editor can act as a proofreader and copyeditor for catching and correcting misspellings, typos and grammar goofs; a fact checker to verify the accuracy of all cited information; and a comprehensive editor who can elaborate on the book's tone and scope. At its most complex, editing can include a structural edit. This means the editor changes the order of content to make it flow from section to section.

An editor is a set of fresh eyes. Don't be offended by their edits. What you write may seem brilliant, but even best-selling authors have editors covering their work. *Raise Your Voice* had four editors.

When choosing an editor, it's important to obtain a sample of their work to find one who suits your book's subject. Once you've chosen an editor, point the editor toward other titles that have a similar writing style to yours. This will give your editor a clearer picture of what you expect. Always define how much and what type of editing you want. If you don't want structural changes, say so. If you need facts checked, mention it.

You can find editors in the **Editor List**. If your budget is tight, many graduate students are willing to edit in exchange for college credit. Now that your book has been edited, let's see if we can spruce it up with pictures and illustrations.

STEP FOUR
Pictures & Illustrations

Pictures and illustrations function as visual guidelines. You can find many by searching for **royalty-free stock photos**. Photos can be purchased very inexpensively, and many are free.

For illustrations and graphs, you can find artists from local high schools and colleges willing to do your artwork just for the recognition. You can find professional artists in the **graphic artists** section.

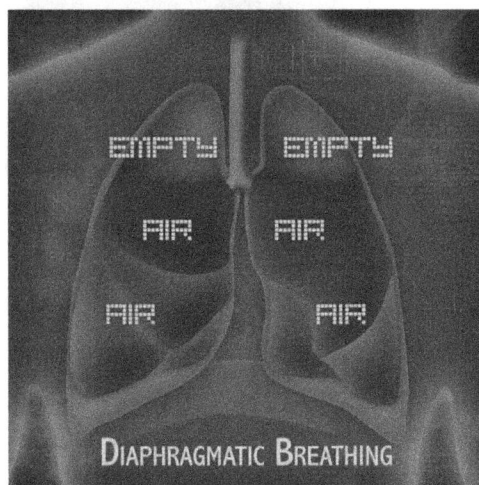

DIAPHRAGMATIC BREATHING

I needed pictures and illustrations in *Raise Your Voice* to explain many concepts. For the first edition, I bartered some music equipment for artwork with a friend. When I released the second edition, I hired a professional illustrator to create anatomical drawings. Unless you're an artist, hire a professional. If you need some artwork, you have two choices:

The first is to search the Internet for artwork similar to what you want. You can purchase millions of stock photos and illustrations from sites listed in the **royalty free stock photos** section. If you're familiar with one of a variety of **photo editing**

programs like Photoshop, you can manipulate an image to your liking.

The second choice is to contact a professional to create a drawing or illustration based on your specifications. The *SpitFire* covers from 711 Press were created by an artist from scratch. If you must have an original drawing and can't do it yourself, hire a professional. A favor from a friend who can draw may cost months of waiting for the final drawing.

Sometimes you'll need pictures of yourself. *Raise Your Voice* is loaded with pictures of me demonstrating vocal techniques. I had several friends take snapshots with a digital camera. For the second edition, I booked time in a photography studio. The professional shots were much better than the amateur snaps.

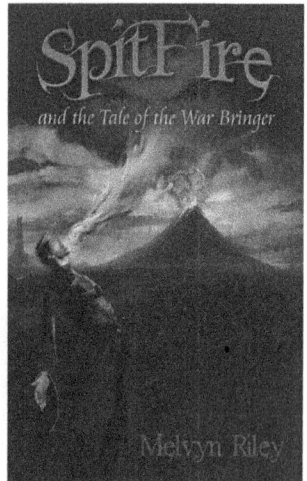

You can find a photographer in your local yellow pages. Contact local studios, visit their offices, review their work, and get pricing. Let them know you need to book only a one- or two-hour session and request that the pictures be transferred to a CD or flash drive. Make sure to tell your photographer they will be listed in the book.

Once you have your images, place each jpeg into your book in its appropriate position. It's a simple "Insert Image" command, which differs from program to program. Unless you're a Photoshop whiz, resizing pictures, adjusting DPI, and making sure the pictures won't bleed black (which makes the printed picture look like it vomited black everywhere) can be a hassle. Unless you master this craft yourself, you can hire an outside book designer, who can also handle image insertion. (More on this in the next chapter.)

When someone else is responsible for image layout, you should pre-place the pictures in the book or add notes to your document, which tells your book designer where you want the pictures. Either way, you must send your designer a folder with the actual images. You can use one of a variety of **file-sending sites** to email the jpegs to your designer.

If you plan to handle image insertion, size each image to fit within the actual page. You might be inserting a jpeg that measures 8.5X11 into a book that is 6X9. If pictures are not resized before insertion, it can turn a 500 KB book into a 30 MB book. This is not a smart move, especially if you plan to release the book in electronic format for readers like Kindle, ePub, or PDF download.

Full-page images, if printed in color, must allow for a .125-inch white border toward the spine, and half-inch margins from which all text must be kept. If ink gets on the spine, the glue won't bind well to the colored ink. Pages could fall out of your book. If fact, a commercial printing company won't even let you fly with something like that.

I inserted low-resolution, untouched, non-resized pictures into Elizabeth Sabine's book *Strengthening Your Singing Voice.* When I received the first printed copy, the images were so dark that it looked like someone had puked black all over the pages. I had to hire a professional to revise the entire book.

To sum up, whenever in need of photographs, illustrations, or charts, if you aren't an experienced artist or photographer, you can buy pictures online, schedule a photo shoot, or find a professional to draw your illustrations. On to Step Five.

STEP FIVE
Interior Book Design

Now *that your book is written and edited,* and your pictures and illustrations are ready to go, it's time for interior book design to create a layout that's pleasing to the eye and ready for printing and digital download. You can do this on your own by studying guides from the **interior design guides** list, or you can hire a professional from the **interior book designers** list.

Formatting the interior of the document includes choosing and embedding the correct fonts for body text, chapter titles, and subtitles; adjusting images; designing headers, footers, and folios ("folio" is publisher speak for page number); determining top, bottom, right, and left margins; and a lot more. Some important factors to consider when formatting the book on your own are:

- Book size
- Margins
- Fonts

BOOK SIZE

Some typical book sizes (in inches) are 8.5X11, 6X9, 5.5X8.5, and 5X8. I suggest that your book match the typical book size for your genre. Book dimensions are usually listed on Internet book sites under the product details. You can also take a small tape measure into a book store and physically measure similar books.

The first edition of *Raise Your Voice* was 8.5X11, like other vocal instruction books on the market. I changed it to 6X9 for the second edition, so that my students could easily slip it into their gig bag.

Set your document to the chosen book size. **Setting page size** within your word processor is easy. If you can't find where to set the book size, refer to the word processor help link.

MARGINS

Margins refer to the blank space on the sides of the book pages. You don't want the edge of your words close to the center of the book or they'll be too hard to read. White space along the top, bottom, and outside edge of the book allows room for page numbers and chapter titles and will ensure that wording isn't cropped during printing. For this book, the margins are as follows:

Top	0.5"
Bottom	0.5"
Left	0.5"
Right	0.5"
Gutter	0.25"
Header	0.5"
Footer	0.5"

Margins will vary depending on the book and the capabilities of the printing company. Another type of spacing listed above is gutter, which allows extra space for the binding, to avoid that "hard-reading" or "glued" situation along the inside edges of the pages.

FONTS

Fonts are a matter of taste. I don't use Times New Roman because it resembles a term paper. There are better choices, such as Georgia, Bookman, and Book Antiqua for the main content, and Arial, Tahoma, Geneva for titles. Unless you've studied book design, your designer will readjust the fonts. I like to set up the book size, margins, and fonts so that I have an idea of the page count. Once I'm finished with my book, I simply hand it over to my book designer, Daniel Middleton, from Scribefreelance.com.

If you prefer to master book design, I suggest studying books listed in the **interior design guides** list. For me it's a creativity drain, so I leave it to Daniel. If you'd like to start with the basics, you can also have your designer create a basic document template for you. Tell them the book size, and they can configure a template with precise margins that can be emailed to you.

A great interior layout is like a nice set of clothes; you wouldn't want to dress like a bum, would you? Authors need to "dress" their book to impress on the inside and out. Speaking of the outside, let's move on to the book cover.

STEP SIX
Designing the Book Cover

THE BOOK COVER SAYS IT ALL

How many times have you grabbed a book off the shelf because the cover caught your eye? Studying book covers is great homework. Head to a local bookstore or library, or browse an online bookstore to review covers on your topic. Which covers do you like? Why? Write down your answers in your **book cover research** template.

Can you create an eye-grabbing cover that explains your topic? *Raise Your Voice* has a picture of me singing into a microphone. That's a smart choice for a vocal training book. *The Ultimate Vocal Workout Diary* is a vocal exercise diary. It has a simplistic diary-type look, with a title that looks as if the words were stitched.

Always tie your book topic into your cover. If you're writing a book on fishing, have some fishing gear on the cover. Look at the *11 Simple Steps* cover. 'Nuff said.

Let's not forget about the spine. We want the book to stand out when stocked on a shelf. I occasionally run my titles on the spine from the bottom up (which is not the norm),

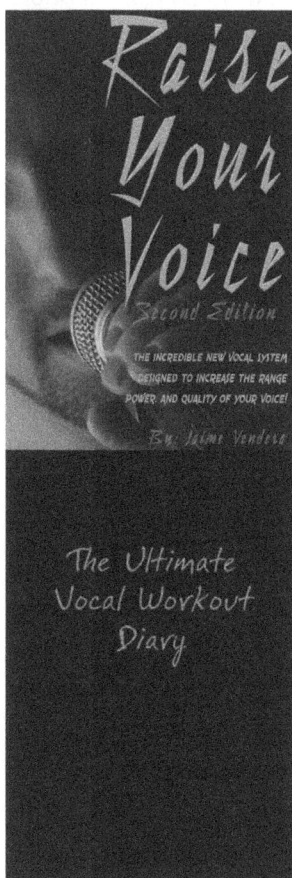

so readers must tilt their heads to the left to read the title. If one of my books is on the shelf among twenty similar books, a person will be forced to pause to review the book.

Don't forget the back cover! The book's description on the back cover is the sales pitch to sell your product. How can you sum up your book and entice the reader to buy in only a few sentences? Read the back covers of books similar to your topic. When writing the description for the back cover, sell your book like it's gold!

You can design the cover yourself in a few hours using a **photo editing program**. When using a printing company, you'll have to use a **book cover template generator** to calculate spine width. A cover must meet the printing specifications, such as color specs, spine width, embedded cover fonts, correct file format, etc. These specs change from printer to printer and must be up-to-date. Covers for ebooks don't require a cover generator template or spine. Many only feature a front cover image. Adding the front and back cover to the ebook is a nice touch, especially when hosting your digital book on sites such as Kindle.

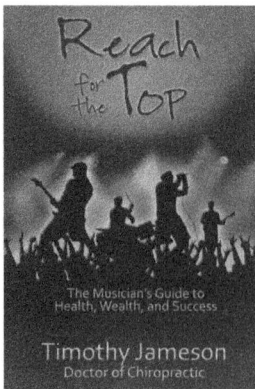

If you use a cover designer, be specific about your expectations. If you don't like their art, don't be afraid to tell them what needs to be changed. If you have an idea for a graphic, hire an illustrator or purchase stock photos online.

My cover design team consists of Molly Burnside and Daniel Middleton. Molly handles Vendera Publishing titles, while Daniel designs all book covers for 711 Press as well as the Vendera Publishing title *Reach for the Top: The Musician's*

Guide to Health, Wealth and Success. They're both listed in my **book cover designers** list.

Finally, if you're going to self-publish, you might consider creating a company logo. Look at the Vendera Publishing logo. It's simple but elegant. A more elaborate logo is my "Jaime Vendera" logo. All white line, but detailed. Other logos are even more elaborate, such as the winding snake logo for RockSource360, created by my graphic designer Benoit Guerville.

Your logo represents your brand. If you plan to release a series of books based on one specific subject such as fishing, the logo should reflect that subject. An illustration of a fishing rod at the end of *Gone Fishin' Publications* would fit well. Be creative. If not creating the logo yourself, share your vision with your illustrator.

While we wait for your cover to be finished, let's move on to the next step, book conversions.

STEP SEVEN
Book Conversions

N*ow, it's time for book conversion.* Most pressing is book conversion for printed books. Most printing companies require a PDF file. Generally, word processors have a simple PDF conversion add-on tool, but if you use it the file may be rejected for errors. I've been rejected for errors such as no page bleed, fonts not embedded, etc. I didn't have time to master a file conversion program, so I hired a professional to convert my document.

There are other types of conversions to consider besides PDF. With ebooks on the rise, you'll want to release your book in other formats such as ePub and .mobi (an Amazon Kindle format).

Ebooks are growing in popularity because they're less expensive than print books, can feature full-color pictures and active website links, and because you can carry hundreds of books on one reader. This means you'll need a second PDF conversion for digital distribution. Other ebook formats follow the rolling page approach or free flow text. For this reason, when converting to formats for readers like the Kindle, it's best not to have page numbers because the document is adjusted to a reader's screen size. Pages are based on wording, not actual page count.

To make this step easy, refer to the **book conversion services** list to find a qualified company for PDF, .mobi, ePub, etc. conversion. If you want to DIY, refer to my **book formatting guides** list.

Once you have your PDF for print and the other formats for various digital outlets, you're ready to publish! Which means we're on to the next step . . .

STEP EIGHT
Publishing Your Book

B<i>efore publishing your book</i> in print and digital forms, let's discuss the differences between published and self-published so you can see why self-publishing is best for you.

A commercial publisher buys the right to publish your book and handles publication, including cover design, book design and production, ISBN number assignment, additional editing, distribution, and marketing. They pay royalties of 6% to 15% after recouping costs and may also pay an advance on royalties. If you receive an advance, you may not see royalties for months until all production costs are covered. If a small percentage works for you, fine. Make sure to read the fine print. Only sign with a company that allows you to retain the rights to your work. If you aren't careful, you could lose ownership of your intellectual property. Understand, however, that it's extremely difficult to get a contract with a commercial publisher. Without an agent, it's nearly impossible. (In a classic catch-22, it's hard to get an agent if you're not already a published author.)

A subsidy publisher or "vanity publisher" will publish your book for a fee (often a hefty one). They also will handle design and production, ISBN number assignment, and, in some instances, distribution and marketing. However, distribution and marketing are generally limited, and some vanity publishers will simply ship the entire print run to you to market and distribute yourself.

A friend of mine, who was published by a well-known company, told me that his first royalty check for his three books, covering a period of six months, was $600. I made the same amount from one self-published book for one month of digital download sales.

Getting a publishing deal is a tough business, and the reward isn't always rewarding. Once your book is published, marketing is the key to success. Your publishing company might put some marketing dollars behind your book but that chance is slim—and the money will come out of your residuals. Why not self-publish, market your book yourself, and retain all profit?

Self-publishing puts you in control because you own the rights to your work and can release your work as a book, ebook, audiobook, DVD, etc. This means YOU retain all the profits. It also means that YOU are responsible for upfront costs including editing, interior/cover design, conversions, purchasing the ISBN number, paying the printing company, getting the book onto Amazon, etc. But, it's easier to accomplish than you think, and the rewards are far greater.

Are you ready to start your publishing company? Here we go:

STARTING YOUR OWN PUBLISHING COMPANY

Becoming a publishing company offers many benefits, especially at tax-time, but requires some groundwork. It's a step-by-step process. To simplify that process, I've broken it into eight steps:

1. Choose a business name
2. Obtain an EIN and state licenses
3. Open a business bank account
4. Open a merchant account
5. Purchase your own ISBN

6. Create a POD and Digital Content account
7. Submit your first book
8. Updating your book information

1. Choose a Business Name

Your business name represents your company. I envisioned my business name as The Voice Connection because my original plan was to write one book, create a website for singers, sell my book, make millions of dollars, and retire by the time I was forty. Once I realized I was having delusions of grandeur, I started a publishing company, Vendera Publishing, and began writing more books.

What name would represent your company best? If you're still writing fishing books, *Gone Fishin' Publications* would be a wise choice.

Once you've chosen your name, the next step is to do an **online company name search** to make sure *Gone Fishin' Publications* isn't in use. Once your name passes muster, you might consider having your company name trademarked through one of the sites listed in **online legal services**. A thorough search will be conducted. If there's a conflict with that name, you'll be notified. I had the name "Vendera" trademarked. Cost-wise, it wasn't outrageous, but it wasn't cheap. It cost me $800 but was well worth it. If you have limited funds, you can trademark at a later date.

2. Obtain an EIN and State Licenses

Your new business requires a business tax I.D. number, also known as an EIN (Employer Identification Number). Your EIN is your permanent number. It states that you are "doing business as" said company, and it can be used immediately for filing federal taxes, opening a bank account, and applying for business loans and licenses.

Filing an EIN is easy. When filing, you must choose your business entity: sole proprietorship, LLC (limited liability company), or corporation. A sole proprietorship is how most new businesses start out and consists of one owner, who is responsible for all debts created by the company. An LLC protects the owner behind the name of the business entity. As a sole proprietor, you are responsible for all debt. An LLC can take on debt without the owner being affected. A corporation such as an S-Corp allows the individual to protect his or her personal assets in the event of business failure. A simple sole proprietorship or partnership doesn't provide this protection. Resources to help you make that decision can be found in the **legal resource guides** list.

Also check local and state laws. Some states require a vendor's license in order to collect state and local taxes for products sold in your state of residence. This includes selling products through a store location, by mail, and online. For more information, Google "How to obtain a vendor's license in (your state)."

3. Open a business bank account

Once you have a business name and EIN, open a business bank account, which is used for all business transactions, including direct deposits from book sales and business purchases. Your bank statement presents a way of keeping track of all business transactions and expenditures, although a wise businessperson will keep their own set of daily records as well. Come tax time, you'll have a full record of money received and spent.

Speaking of tax time, there are many author and publisher tax deductions, including deductions for computer equipment, phone calls, printing paper, postage, book printing expenditures, Internet expenditures, office space, hiring professionals for book editing, illustrations, or creating book covers, etc. Always pay for business expenses through your business account in order to have an official record of all business transactions.

If you keep a record of all expenditures, you'll be surprised at the difference your business deductions will make on your tax return. For further information, check out the **tax guides for publishers** link.

Back to business—to set up a new account, go to your local bank and apply for a business account. Your bank will require your EIN, so have it with you. You can start a business account for as little as $50.

4. Open a Merchant Account

Years ago, you had to nearly sell your soul to set up a merchant account. It's much easier now with sites like PayPal, Google Checkout, and ClickBank, which have made it easy to accept online payments. With innovative companies like Square, you can now process credit cards right on your smart phone.

Like any standard merchant account, a fee is applied with every transaction. These fees are relatively small, and you aren't charged other monthly fees unless you elect to use other professional features. Refer to the **merchant account** list to review and choose a provider.

Once you've chosen a merchant account, you can send and receive money via the Internet. Deposits can be wired to your bank account, but most online accounts will require you to link to your bank account.

5. Purchase Your Own ISBN

Before your book can be sold in print, you'll need an International Standard Book Number. An ISBN refers to a series of thirteen numbers that uniquely identifies books published internationally. You must have an ISBN to sell your print book, though many digital download sites, such as Amazon's KDP (Kindle Direct Publishing), assign unique identifiers to the book, which means an ISBN isn't required. Go to the **ISBN setup** link to begin the process.

6. Create a POD and Digital Content Account

When self-publishing, you'll need a POD (print on demand) book printer. A POD company offers printing options such as one book at a time or mass printing. My POD company, Lightning Source, can print as few or as many books as needed and also handles book distribution to websites like amazon.com. You should choose a POD company over an *offset printer*, which requires the purchase of a large quantity of books per order. Offset printers ship books directly to you, which means you have to store and distribute them to customers and online bookstores, whereas a POD will handle the entire process for you.

There are many POD choices listed under **POD companies**. Research each company to consider factors such as new title setup fees, cost per book for print, whether you must order a *proof,* etc. A proof is the first printed copy of your book for review. Once you've reviewed and approved your proof, it will be released to multiple online bookstores.

You also need to decide where to sell your ebooks. You can sell them through your own site as well as through Google, Amazon, and Barnes & Noble, to name a few. When choosing a POD company, refer to their digital distribution channels to see if it's feasible for your printing company to handle all distribution. Otherwise, refer to the **digital content companies** list to set up individual accounts that you will handle. Now, let's launch that book!

7. Submit Your First Book

Now that you're an official publisher, have your own business bank account, purchased ISBN numbers, have established a merchant account, and created your POD and digital distribution accounts, let's submit your book for distribution. Follow the **POD upload guidelines** and **digital content upload guidelines** provided by each account to submit your book. Printing and digital content companies have strict guidelines concerning the interior and cover that must be followed. Study the specifications before submitting. If your interior or cover fails to pass specs, pass the email you received along to your interior or cover designer. They will correct the errors.

During this step, you'll need to price your book. I suggest you review the pricing of books in your genre. You can go to amazon.com and type in key words to review similar books. For example, I would type in "vocal instruction" and review at least ten books that are similar to mine, noting page count, pricing, and any extras such as CDs, DVDs, downloads, etc.

A good threshold for profit is $2 to $4 per book. If you've reviewed similar books and factored in the competition, you'll realize this is the norm. You don't want to price yourself out of market. A $2 to $4 threshold allows you to play with discount percentage to other bookstores. If you make $2 at a 55% discount, you'll have to play around with that discount at holidays like Christmas and on Black Friday. Throughout the year, you can maintain a discount as low as 20% (though 40%

will help get you into library catalogs) and bump it to 55% during holidays for bookstores to lower the price for more sales.

To calculate your residual per book, you must factor printing, shipping, and handling costs. If your printing cost and fees are $5, do the math to figure out the $2 to $4 threshold.

When pricing ebooks, I at least deduct the amount of the printing cost to create a new price. This allows both a price break and quick delivery. Again, if you sell the ebook yourself, you retain all profit. If selling through another distribution chain in another format—Amazon Kindle/.mobi for example—the price per book may be substantially lower than the print version. Check pricing on each format and adjust accordingly.

If you want to increase sales through your website, offer a book/ebook combination at a reduced price. For example:

Raise Your Voice 2nd Edition

Book	$29.95
Ebook	$24.95
Total	$54.90

Book/Ebook Combination $44.90 ($10.00 discount)

8. Updating Book Information

To protect your intellectual property and also help libraries and other outlets find your books, perform the following steps:

1. **List your book on My Identifiers.** Once your book is launched, go to myidentifiers.com to upload your book information and cover. I let this slide my first few books. When I went into the

system I found mistakes, including one of my books being registered as a Simon and Schuster title, two books with switched ISBN numbers, one book labeled as an ebook of another title, and one that cost me an ISBN. Learn more at **setting up my title at Bowkerlink.**

2. **Join PCN.** On the copyright page of a book published by major publishing companies, you'll see Cataloging-in-Publication (CIP) data, followed by the book's details, including ISBN, Library of Congress control number, etc. These control numbers are used by libraries across the country to easily input the data into their local library system or database, thus cataloging the book in-house. The PCN system is the self-published-author equivalent of the big publishers' CIP system with the Library of Congress. Having an LCCN allows your book to be searchable on the Library of Congress site, easily cataloged by libraries. Refer to the **PCN setup** for more details.

3. **Check book sites for proper information.** It's important that your book be represented correctly on any website that sells it. Potential problems include missing information (such as the description of the book), typos, incorrect page count, and no cover image. If you find errors, contact your POD company rep, and then contact each digital content company you're using. Many sites, including Amazon, allow you to correct errors through your Author Central account. (Author Central covered later.)

4. **Copyrighting your book.** Once your book is released, submit a copy to the copyright office for copyright protection. The newest revisions to the copyright laws state that you own your work the minute you write it. But it's still wise to be protected in all ways possible, including adding a © symbol on the copyright page at the beginning of your book. To copyright your book, go to the **copyrighting your book** link.

Now that you've published your book, the easy part is over. Now it's time to develop a business plan, build your website, market your book, and, most important, develop book-related products and workshops for multiple streams of income. Let's move on to the next chapter.

STEP NINE
Multiple Streams of Income

Writing one book won't make you rich! But once you become an author, it can lead to multiple streams of income, including speaking engagements, workshops, radio shows, and television appearances. Before you even build your website, you must consider these multiple streams, as they will affect the content of your site. Let's start by discussing book revenue.

BOOK REVENUE

If you take advantage of all possible book revenue streams, you'll have multiple sources paying you per month. If you sell your books through your website, you retain the profit minus printing costs, digital storage costs, merchant account fees, and website hosting costs. If you sell your books at a workshop, you'll owe a percentage to the facility, unless discussed otherwise, such as a rental fee only for the facility. In the case of a book signing, if the store pre-purchases your books, they will retain all profit. If you supply your books, you will owe a percentage of your sales to the bookstore. If your book retails at $15 and costs $5 to print, your profit will be $10 per book minus percentage of sales owed to the bookstore. Book-signing fees can vary from 20% to 60%, most likely in favor of the bookstore.

Other print book revenue is received via your POD company, which functions as a broker house, offering your books to bookstores worldwide. If you allow a 50% discount, which brings your $15 book revenue down $7.50 minus the $5 printing fee, your final revenue is $2.50 per book. This seems low, but there's no sense writing a great book and then selling only a few copies through your website just because you wish to retain full profit.

Revenue from downloadable products = very little overhead; no upfront costs, no inventory, and no printing expense. All you need is a website and the means to send the product, including via a server listed in the **digital storage** list. Once an ebook is sold, you'll receive notification and the buyer receives a download link.

You'll recall from the last step that I suggested a profit of $2 to $4 per book. There are exceptions to this rule. For example, *Raise Your Voice 2nd Edition* is $29.95. That's steeper than your typical vocal instruction book, but mine includes 400 pages, more than ten hours of downloadable audio and video instruction, free vocal exercises, and a *Raise Your Voice* member's section with bonuses and a message board.

By offering extras that are accessible only through your book, you can raise the price. It's important to note that all my bonuses are digital downloads. This keeps my price per book down. If I included CDs and DVDs with the book, I would have doubled, if not tripled, my price, possibly costing sales.

Offering downloadable bonuses with your book is a way to get people to your website. More traffic equals more sales. Once a person visits a website to download book bonuses, there's a chance they'll purchase other products listed on the website.

Can you offer downloadable bonuses with your book? All you need to create audio recordings or instructional videos is a microphone, a webcam, and some **video and audio capturing/editing software**. You'll simply upload your new files to your website (more on this later) and make sure your readers know it exists. Always mention the bonuses on the book sales page and at the beginning of your book. Here's an excerpt from *Raise Your Voice*:

CONGRATULATIONS!
You are now a member of an elite group.

This book comes with lifetime free access to the Raise Your Voice Members section.

The Members section contains all of the audio examples from this book, downloadable vocal exercises, a message board to discuss the techniques, and hours of instructional videos to guide you through the <u>Raise Your Voice</u> *system.*

Enjoy!

To access the Members section, go to:
www.raiseyourvoicebook.com or
www.thevoiceconnection.com
From the home page, click on "Members."

The password is . . . buy my book to find out, ha-ha.

Now that you've increased revenue by offering book bonuses, let's expand our product line.

Video. Every book can be turned into a video. Simply read through your book, make bullet points, and turn those into video. This is how I created the *Beyond the Voice* video series.

Audio. I created an audio series for screaminglessons.com based on several teaching concepts in my singing books. You can create audio and video products using the tools from the **video and audio capturing/editing software** list.

Workshops. Can you teach people in a live situation how to do what you do in your book? See **workshop tools.**

Speaking Engagements. Now that you're an author, you're considered an expert. I've been hired to break glass with my voice for events as well as perform on television shows around the world. I'm very comfortable in front of a crowd, and I've shared my performance tips in my books. If you're nervous in public, refer to the **public speaking tools** list.

So, what should you charge for audio and video products, workshops, and speaking engagements? Pricing will vary widely. Study the pricing of audio/video products, workshops, and speaking engagements in your genre. The more renowned you become, the more you can demand for speaking engagements and workshops. Don't get greedy at this point. Set your price lower and consider it an opportunity to craft your skills. And now, it's finally time for that website.

STEP TEN
Time for a Website

As an author, *marketing yourself* as an expert in your field is crucial. Your website is a multifaceted branding platform for selling your products, storing your book bonuses, and posting your bio, videos, blogs, latest news, and more.

First, you'll need a domain name. I wanted to purchase voiceconnection.com, but it was already taken, so I chose thevoiceconnection.com. I've also purchased domain names to mask my affiliate links. For my Xooma affiliate, I chose singerswater.com to mask my affiliate link. Before moving on, decide on your domain name. Next, check availability and purchase if available. If not, pick a similar title. For **purchasing web domains**, scroll the list to choose where to buy.

Purchase a .com name as it's the most recognizable. I don't think you need anything but .com, but I also bought jaimevendera.net. You never know when others will try to steer people away from your site by launching one with a similar name.

Companies have emailed trying to sell similar domain names. For example, I host vocal coach Elizabeth Sabine's website. Since elizabethsabine.com was unavailable, I chose elizabethsabine.net. Coincidentally, as I started working on this section, I got an email from a company trying to sell me elizabethsabine.com for nearly $600. Here's my reply:

I am getting ready to release my fifth book. This particular book is about self-publishing. What's funny is *that I JUST wrote a section on the sharks and swindlers out there who scavenge the Internet buying up similar domain names and then try to sell them to people like me for a quick buck. Wow, you are only asking a mere $557? How ridiculous. I want to thank you for reinforcing my decision to steer all of my readers away from people who offer this shady service.*

Steer clear of domain name vultures; they're only looking to scam the naïve victim. You can find a name that will work for you. Dot-coms are the most memorable to choose from, but if your creativity fails you, .net, .org, .biz, and .info are suitable choices.

Once you've secured your name, you'll need to browse the **hosting servers** to choose your website hosting platform. A server allows you to build, maintain, and add content to your website. If you're considering a free hosting site, read the fine print. Free sites post banners for other companies. This looks amateur. The only free exception I like is a blogging site. You can start a blog and use it as your website, though it limits the bells and whistles. Check out the **blogging platforms** list to make a decision.

CREATING THE WEBSITE
Technology is rapidly evolving, so a webmaster isn't always the best choice. With website platforms like Squarespace, AmericanAuthor, and Website Tonight, it's easy for almost anyone to build their own website. For a full list, check out **CMS platforms**.

Both 711Press.com and VenderaPublishing.com were built on Squarespace.com without the need of a webmaster. If you have absolutely no experience, a good webmaster can get your site up and running. A good webmaster can build specific graphics or tweak the available templates. Check out the **webmaster/web designers** list for help.

A great-looking website requires planning. You must carefully think through the design, including colors, fonts, video, images, etc. The goal of your website is to convey your specific message to your audience. Write a list of what you want your viewers to understand, learn, and remember when they visit your site. For example, the goals of 711Press.com are:

- Demonstrate our innovative approach to publishing
- Let people know how to contact us
- Provide examples of our work
- Express what is different and desirable about our publishing model

Other options that you, as an author, might require include:

- Book description and author bio page
- Online media press kit for booking radio show
- Shopping cart for purchasing books or ebooks
- Message board or blog to allow visitors to comment
- Media player that plays videos or music
- Password-protected membership area
- Video room/video downloads
- Chat room

All these options are important, especially the blog, which keeps your site updated with new material. If your website doesn't have blogging capabilities, you can sign up for one listed under **blogging platforms**.

When blogging, use keywords that relate to your topic and plant these keywords, aka meta-tags, through your website. Tags are important for drawing traffic. You'll find the best tags related to your topic under the **metatag tracking sites** list. What makes for a good blog? Interviews with experts in your field and free tips or lessons related to your book in the form of text, audio, or video. The worst thing you can do is build a website and let it stagnate. Visitors won't return if the site is dead.

Once you have the general idea for what your site needs to convey, categorize the information. Most content can be organized in several ways:

- By the type of audience that would want that type of information (For Beginning Students, For Experts, For Media)
- By the main subject area (Writing, Usability, Social Networking)
- By activity (Learn More, Purchase a Book, Contact Us)
- By typically recognized web areas (Home, About Us, FAQ, Our Products/Services, Contact Us)

A concise, easy to maneuver website is vital. If someone is searching your site for a particular piece of information, they must know what section of your site to visit. If you make people hunt for information, you'll lose valuable customers.

Once you have an organizational scheme, make some sketches of how you want your site laid out. If you're building the site yourself via a CMS platform, browse the available templates provided with the hosting plan to find a similar scheme. Most templates can be customized.

If you don't see a template you like, incorporate other forms of website coding such as Joomla, which broadens your template options with a variety of edgier designs. Refer to the **website templates** list to find a better template.

Now you're ready to build. If you choose the webmaster route and are on a tight budget, you might find a willing web design student from a college. Be clear about what you're willing to pay and how soon you expect the site to go live.

Now you must gather graphics, pictures, the book description, your author bio, and press releases. You also need to choose a shopping cart platform, add a message board (if required), add your merchant account info for accepting payment, set up an email address, and so on. You should already have a merchant account such as PayPal, which can be added to your website. Many merchant sites have a shopping cart option. For other choices, visit the **shopping carts** list. For message boards, select a service from the **message boards** list if your platform doesn't provide this service.

You want a great-looking website that can be viewed on a variety of browsers as well as on a smartphone and tablet. Once you've released your book, created a few new products, and launched your website, it's time for the last step: marketing that book to make it a best seller! Let's move on.

STEP ELEVEN
Marketing Madness

Sadly, most authors think that once the book is published, it will fly off the shelves—false. The success of your book relies on marketing. Don't let the word scare you, because marketing can be fun and rewarding.

I've made it fun by creating the Super Simple Book Marketing System, or "SSBMS" for short. The SSBMS is nothing new. I've simply combined marketing strategies into a straightforward system based on free tactics to market your book. There's much an author can do to promote a book without spending a dime, while avoiding hiring expensive companies to market for you.

Authors are led astray by companies that make a lot of promises: They'll skyrocket your website to the top of the rankings, give you access to email lists with thousands of people begging to buy your book, and show you how to sell a million books. In reality, the only people getting rich are the ones offering these services. I've bought into several marketing schemes over the years, including buying email lists, blasting millions of "subscribers," hiring marketing companies, purchasing keywords, purchasing banner space, using automated marketing software. None of the paid options made a difference to my book sales. So let's get started—for free.

SSBMS is interactive and will work only by doing it! Slowly work through this chapter step by step, never moving on until you finish an assignment. As you work through the SSBMS, keep track of contact information such as website and email addresses. I suggest that you:

1. Create a folder in your web browser labeled "Author websites." Don't bookmark websites you'll visit frequently in the general folder because your bookmarks will become lost in the shuffle. Bookmark every site mentioned in this chapter in your new folder.

2. As you explore new websites, save contact information and sign-in information for websites you join in a document on your desktop labeled "Author Information." Now, on with the show.

STEP ONE: THE PRESS RELEASE

A press release is the sales pitch for your book, meant to announce the release and captivate your potential audience. Before submitting a press release, you must write one.

Assignment #1—Write Your Press Release

The press release sums up the book in a few paragraphs and may contain a picture of the author and book, plus an author bio. Learn how to write your press release by following the **press release examples**.

Once your press release is written, the SSBMS focuses on submitting it to several major news outlets including local newspapers, television stations, press release sites, magazines, and book review sites. Let's start with newspapers.

Assignment #2—Collecting Newspaper Contacts

Begin collecting contacts for every local newspaper within a fifty-mile radius of your home. You can browse the yellow pages or search on google.com. In the Google toolbar, type "Your County (or city), Your State: Newspapers." For example, type "Orange County, California: Newspapers." Using the colon tells Google to narrow the search. If you type "Orange County, California, Newspapers," your search could bring up links to websites that relate to "Oranges," anything to do with "California," and links to "newspapers" from all over the United States.

Another choice is to use onlinenewspapers.com. Use their database to search by city and state. (Don't forget to bookmark this website in your new browser folder.)

Once you've located the local newspaper contact information, including names, numbers, and email addresses, transfer the info into your **newspaper contacts** list.

Track down newspapers in the largest cities in your state as well.

Assignment #3—Gather Television Contacts

Any local news station within a 50-mile radius of your base of operation should know about your book release. If there are bigger cities outside that radius but within a few hours' travel time, gather their contact information as well.

In the Google toolbar, type "County or City, State: television stations." For example, "Louisville, Kentucky: television stations." Copy all contact info into the **television contacts** list.

Now that you have a nice list of contact information, we're close to sending out a press release. But first, answer one simple question. "What do you have that's newsworthy?"

Assignment #4—What Do You Have That's Newsworthy?

News outlets want compelling, interesting stories. "Local author releases new book" is good, but your contacts will be more responsive if you captivate them even before they open your email. Here's how.

When I finished the second edition of *Raise Your Voice*, I used my notoriety as a glass-shattering MythBuster to pitch my press release. In the email header, I added, "Glass-shattering world-record-holding singer reveals his secrets in new book."

Always find a unique edge to pitch your press release. What are your attributes? Why did you write the book? What is unique about your book? Use that information to create a catchy, attention-grabbing email header, and then move on to the next assignment.

Assignment #5—Crafting Your Email

Captivating email header—check. Now it's time to write the awe-inspiring body. Both header and body need to be slim and to the point. Your goal is to catch the recipient's attention quickly. Speaking of slim, keep the header to less than twenty words. Less is better. A header such as *"Local first-time author releases* Gone Fishin, *the new book that explains the secrets used to quadrupling his daily catch"* could pique some interest. But a header like *"Author catches fifty bass in eight hours, shares his secrets in new book"* is better and shorter.

The header hooks the fish, and the email body reels them in because it contains the newsworthy story. When writing the body of the email, keep it short—one to three paragraphs. Newsrooms don't have time for your life story. Here is an example of a press release email:

Dear John,

My name is Jaime Vendera. I'm writing to inquire about

submission guidelines for local news. I'm a local author who watches WXYZ every night during dinner. I'm also a world renowned vocal coach, most known for my ability to shatter glass with my voice, as seen on shows like MythBusters. *In fact, I was dubbed an honorary MythBuster by the hosts. My latest book on vocal training,* Raise Your Voice Second Edition, *has been endorsed by many well-known rock singers. I'd like to let my community know about the release of my new book, and I'd be happy to share a few stories about my adventures as an honorary MythBuster.*

Sincerely,

Jaime Vendera
Author of Raise Your Voice
JaimeVendera.com
740-531-2122

Take advantage of your email signature, including "God Bless" or "Sincerely," your name, the name of your book, and your contact information. Once you've finished your header and email, move on to the next assignment:

Assignment #6—Releasing the Press Release

Individually email everyone on your contact list, personally addressing each email to the appropriate person at each company. Always add the contact name, newspaper/TV station name, TV call letters, etc. Being personable will increase your chances of being picked up by the local news.

Double-check your email for typos. No one likes deciphering

misspelled words, or worse, being referred to by the wrong name, newspaper, or radio station.

Once you've blasted your list, adopt the following highlighting system:

Yellow = Contacted
Red = Confirmed
Blue = Completed

Highlight the contact in yellow once you've sent the email. Re-highlight a contact in red once you've received a reply. Once the story has run, re-highlight the contact in blue. How do you highlight in a document? Every program is different, but there should be a simple highlighting tool in the tool bar.

Once the story has appeared, follow up with a thank-you email. Finish the email by asking if you can contact again for future news and book releases. Keep the free press door open for future opportunities.

Assignment #7—Internet Press Release Sites

Local newspapers and TV stations were just a warm-up. Are you ready to go global with your press release? Your next assignment is to visit the **press release sites** list. Most are free, but I've listed sites that distribute for a small fee. Go to each site one by one and fill out the submission form, add your press release, and hit SEND.

Extra Credit

Search online for more press release sites. You should continue to add contacts to your templates and grow your contact list. Now we need to get people reading the book and then get them to tell us what they think. Next stop, book reviews.

Assignment #8—Finding Reviewers

Book reviews are crucial for an author's success. Remember those gold nuggets? Our goal is to find readers interested in reviewing your book. The best resources for book reviewers include book clubs, discussion sites, and magazines/ezines. Before moving on, I suggest ordering a dozen copies of your book, because you'll have to send out printed copies when requested. Most review sites accept digital submissions, but some reviewers prefer print versions. The cost of sending out a few free books is worth a great review. Kindle gifts are a good choice too. Now it's time to get started.

Use Google to search for topic-related magazines. I've searched for singing magazines by typing in keywords such as "singers: magazines." Our fishing author would Google "fishing: magazines."

There are now thousands of online magazines, known as ezines. You should also use "ezines" in place of "magazines" when performing a search. When you find magazine/ezine sites related to your subject, copy and paste the website name, web address, contact name, email address, and phone number into your **magazine/ezine contacts** list.

Assignment #9—Submit to Your Magazine/Ezine List

It's time to submit an email to your magazines/ezines contacts to ask if they accept books for review. Don't be surprised if you're contacted for an interview as well. Take advantage of all exposure.

Assignment #10—Submit to the Following Sites

Let's review what we've accomplished so far:

Newspapers √
TV stations √
Press release websites √
Magazines/Ezines √

Now it's time to contact sites that are specifically dedicated to book reviews. Go to the **book review sites** list and submit to the sites I've listed.

Google *"your topic* book reviews," such as "fishing book reviews," to find more reviewers. This will not exactly give you a listing of submission services, but it can lead you to people and blogs that review books. Also search amazon.com. Many Amazon reviewers have their contact info listed on their personal Amazon page. Find reviewers for your genre and contact them for a review.

Assignment #11—Collect Reviews and News Clippings

Gather great book reviews, newspaper clippings, and live video of you. Request that copies be sent to you digitally and ask for permission to post them in your blog and on your site. Cite the source of each article, review, or video footage, including the author, company name, and website.

We've finally wrapped up Step One of the SSBMS. It seems like tons of research, but if you take a moment to reflect on what you've accomplished, I guarantee you'll smile! No time for a breather, let's move on to Step Two:

STEP TWO: MAKING NEW FRIENDS

By participating in book discussions, reviewing books, and joining discussion boards, you'll spread the word about your book and expertise. People appreciate expert advice and love making friends with experts. Speaking of which, I have one condition for this step: When visiting the following sites, don't think of yourself as an author; think of yourself as an expert!

Assignment #12—Join the Following Sites

The purpose of Step Two is to become interactive. Just remember to be professional in your interactions. Go to the **author sites** list, join each site, and become active in each community.

Assignment #13—Don't Over-Participate

Participate in a chat or book discussion when you can add to the discussion. When posting, double-check your posts so that you express yourself clearly. NEVER come across as arrogant. The written word can sound insensitive at times. There's no need to start an online argument.

With that said, you will run into arrogant people potentially aiming to stir trouble. Don't get caught up in an unnecessary argument. Nobody wins except the soul-sucking leeches that start the argument. Arguing will only upset you, waste time, and drain your energy.

Before posting, read the rules of the site to make sure your post will not be considered spam. Focus on contributing useful information. I personally think it best not to mention your book in a post. When I read posts like, *Oh, I've had that happen before. I explain how to overcome that situation in my book "I'm a Genius," which you can buy at imagenius.com,* I leave the conversation. It's classier to post the name of your book in your signature such as:

Jaime Vendera
Author of Raise Your Voice

If you're the author of several books on multiple subjects, only list the book in your signature that relates to the topic being discussed. In other words, only list your singing books in your signature on a singing discussion, etc. I'd never sign, "Author of *11 Simple Steps*" in my signature on a vocal technique discussion board. Now, go do some posting and have some fun!

Extra Credit

Start a message board on your website.

We've come to the end of Step Two. You've been prepping for Step Three and had no clue. Welcome to the world of interviews. Let's proceed.

STEP THREE: INTERVIEWS

If interviews make you nervous, fear not; nervousness is easily overcome. Here are a few tips to conquer interview anxiety and master public speaking:

Tip #1—Talk as if you're talking with a friend. I used to become nervous before interviews until I had the chance to speak to a DJ several hours before one particular interview. We hit it off because we both loved singing. He made the comment that he wished he'd recorded our conversation because it would have made for a great interview. He told me he'd had many interviews with nervous people, as revealed by their shaky voices, mumbling, talking too fast, speaking inaudibly, or just being boring.

His ideal interview was a knowledgeable person with an upbeat attitude who presented through clear, properly paced, audible speech. In the past, I'd exemplified each type of interview he detested. When you do an interview, be yourself. Pretend it's a typical conversation with no one else listening. Once you loosen up, you'll shine.

Tip #2—Offer free ebooks to your listeners. I know I said to pretend no one was listening, but people will be listening, so turn listeners into fans by offering free copies of your ebook. If you're on a show that includes call-ins, pose a question and invite listeners to call with the answer. Give a free ebook to the first caller with the correct answer. (Discuss this with the interviewer before the show.) This costs you nothing and is free promotion. If the show doesn't feature call-ins, offer freebies to listeners if they join your website or sign up for your mailing list within 24 hours. Add that they MUST mention the name of the radio station.

Tip #3—Offer other freebies for following your blog. Create a special report, based on part of your book, which a listener can download for free when signing up for your mailing list. This report can be a simple one-page PDF covering one topic from your book. If they don't own your product, the free report will draw them to your product line.

Tip #4—NEVER end a show without summing up. ALWAYS sum up the interview by mentioning your book and website at the end of the show. If the website can be misspelled, vocally spell out the name of the website during the show. Jaimevendera.com is often misspelled, so I always spell my name. You have a small window of opportunity to gain new clients. Never miss the chance to point them to your website where they can buy your products and schedule consultations.

Radio interviews play an important role in book sales and only require four simple ingredients:

1. A great radio press kit in order to get booked on the show
2. A story to be told
3. Great speaking skills
4. Your time to do the show.

Most interviews can be done by phone, so you don't even have to leave the house. If you still feel you need to brush up on your speaking skills and conquer the jitters, check out the **public speaking and stage fright tools** list.

Assignment #14—Gathering Radio Contacts

You can't do interviews without having radio station contacts, so head back to Google to search for radio stations in your niche. I search for radio stations with keywords such as "rock music: radio stations." Get more specific by including your "area" or adding "online" as a keyword. For example, our fishing author can type "fishing: online radio stations: California" to find an entire list of online radio stations in California that discuss fishing.

Begin this assignment by searching for local radio stations within a 100-mile radius of your home. After you've made a list of local stations, search for online radio stations. With the creation of sites like blogtalkradio.com, online radio is growing. Add your contacts to your **radio interview contacts** list.

You can buy lists for radio station contacts, but why pay for what you can find for free with a bit of work? Contact information is always changing, so that $99 list of 1,000 contacts may produce 300 invalid contacts, 400 contacts that don't review artists in your field, and 200 contacts that are radio stations that run at three in the morning. That leaves you with a list of 100 possibly usable contacts. You can easily find lists of hundreds of contacts just on one website, for free, within minutes. People love hearing stories early in the morning on their way to work, during lunch, and on the drive home.

Assignment #15—Creating a Radio Press Kit

Before contacting radio stations, you'll need an amazing press kit, which contains all the vital information a radio host would need to know about you, your book, and your area of expertise. A press kit can include previous book reviews, celebrity endorsements, statistics related to your book subject, a list of topics of interest, and sample questions the host can ask during the interview. Your press kit must contain:

*Your bio with picture

*Brief description of your book(s) with cover picture

*Endorsements from experts/celebrities if you've obtained any at this point. If not, contact experts in your field by email, phone, agent, etc. Send copies of your book, get the endorsement, and add it to your press kit. Nothing beats a great endorsement.

*Hot topics that can be discussed on the radio show during your interview.

*A list of sample questions for the DJ. This streamlines the interview, because you've laid the groundwork. By doing their job for them, they won't have to spend time researching you. You'll make it a no-brainer, easy show.

*Additional bonuses you can add to your online press kit are fun facts concerning your book subject as well as media clips and articles.

Your press kit should come in two forms: A static PDF and virtual press kit that's hosted on a website such as any of the **virtual press kit sites** and one hosted on your website. The advantages of an online press kit over a PDF file is that it can come alive on the page, with video book trailers, audio/video messages from the author, and photo albums. Give the interviewer both options. Check out my **sample press kit** and feel free to use mine as a template.

Assignment #16—Booking Radio Shows
For this assignment, you'll:

A. Contact all local radio station contacts via email;
B. Contact one Internet radio station per day during the rest of this chapter.

Use the same email techniques for contacting newspapers, televisions, and magazines. Remember to craft that captivating header and enticing email to grab the recipient's attention. Attach your press kit PDF, your ebook, and a link to your online press kit for review. Here is an example email I've used to book radio shows to promote my vocal techniques.

Show Topic Ideas from an honorary glass shattering MythBuster (email header)

Hello John,

My name is Jaime Vendera. I am a world-renowned vocal coach, who is most known for my ability to shatter glass with my voice, as seen on shows like MythBusters. (In fact, I was dubbed an honorary MythBuster by the hosts, Adam and Jaime.) I train professional singers in power and stamina techniques for surviving on the road and maintaining their speaking voice during interviews. My books on vocal training and positive reinforcement have been read by musicians, singers, and writers worldwide. I think I have many topics that would be of great interest to listeners of KNAC's Morning Rock Show, such as:

*How to become a MythBuster

*How to shatter glass with your voice

*Voice related topics, such as "singing in the car," "morning warm up tips," "extending your vocal range," and "can the speaking voice hurt the singing voice?"

*How to train with a rock star

How to become a rock star

Unblocking writer's block

Accomplishing your goals and dreams

I've attached my profile for your staff to review. Feel free to email me at any time. I would be more than happy to email you a copy of "Raise Your Voice Complete" which is my three-book vocal training system, as well as "Unleashing Your Creative Mindset," which is my book that explains the method I used to set a world record, become a MythBuster best-selling author and one of the world's top vocal coaches. I can't wait to hear from you.

Sincerely,

Jaime Vendera
JaimeVendera.com
740-531-2122

In the old days of radio, a person submitted their press kit by mail while trying to figure out ways to make their unsolicited package stand out among the fifty others piled up on the station manager's desk. I'm sure authors sent hundreds of bright red packages with a copy of their book, printed bio, and glossy 8X10 mug shot. Can you spell EXPENSIVE? With technology at our fingertips, we can create an incredibly attractive and impressive online press kit that would blow away its physical counterpart. Cost to mail one press kit with book: $10 and up. Cost to email a link to your electronic press kit: $0.

Now it's go time. Email all local radio stations today and one Internet station per day. It will take only five to ten minutes. Remember to use your highlighting system when contacting your list.

*Join the sites listed in **interview experts** list.*

STEP FOUR: SOCIAL NETWORKING

Social networking is another form of interactive and free marketing.

Assignment #17—Joining Social Networking Sites

New social networking sites pop up every day. I listed some of the top ones in the **social networking sites** list. Join and utilize the sites that cater to your book.

The power of phone apps is exploding. You might consider creating a phone app for your website. Search Google for key phrases such as "social media apps development" or "app development software." You'll find sites and software programs that you can use to develop apps both for free and for a price.

*Use QT codes to increase sales. Learn more on the **QT codes** list.*

STEP FIVE: HANGING OUT AT AMAZON

Your Amazon author account is a social networking platform you MUST utilize. If you don't have an author account, it's time to create one.

Assignment #18—Creating Your Amazon Account

Go to authorcentral.amazon.com to create an Author Central account. It's a social networking platform, right on Amazon, designed to keep your readers up-to-date on future releases, book tours, etc. Once you've created an author page, add your bio and pictures of you and your books, update your book description, and add blog posts.

> *If you post reviews on Amazon, edit your signature to include your name and "author of . . ." When you review books and participate in Amazon discussions, people will remember your name and associate it with your book. Once you've set up your profile, begin implementing the following Amazon assignments:*

Assignment #19—Search Inside the Book

Upload your book to the Search Inside program. Search Inside is like going to a bookstore, allowing people to flip through a book before they buy it. Some authors have frowned on this program, feeling it's giving away free access to their book. I disagree. If you allow potential buyers to browse your book, they're more likely to buy it. If the program doesn't improve sales, you can easily remove your book from the program at any time. Go to **search inside** to sign up. Follow the guidelines to submit your book.

Assignment #20—Become a Reviewer

Reviewing books builds your credibility as a trusted authority on Amazon. The beauty of reviewing other books and products is that you have a chance to promote your book with every review, because your Amazon signature features your name and book title.

Start by reviewing books and products you've purchased. Continue reviewing items you buy or own, including music, books, videos, etc. To find the list of items you've purchased, refer to the **amazon product purchases** list.

Before posting your first review, let me give you a few tips. First, never leave an intentionally bad review. You wouldn't want someone posting a bad review on your book. There are some 1-star reviews on a few of my books that were planted intentionally. I know because it's the only review the person has ever posted. Leaving a bad review on a competitor's book will backfire on you and drive traffic away from your own book page! With that said, I'm not saying you shouldn't post honest reviews. If there are things about a particular book that you didn't like, post it. It can help the author improve their book.

Once you've reviewed a product, tag the book in the "Tag This Product" area. You can also tag similar books with your book title and post descriptions to your meta-tag suggestions on the "Help Others Find This Item" link. By having your book listed in the tags of similar books, the Amazon search engine will list your book in similar book categories. The more tags you add (maximum of fifteen per book), the higher your book could rate in specific book categories. FYI: Amazon buyers don't just buy one book on a subject; they buy multiple books on a subject.

You cannot review your own book, but you can tag it. Make sure to tag your own book! No one will find your book if you don't set it up to be found. Which brings up another point: Have your friends and family review your book. More reviews will improve your book ranking.

Assignment #21—Join Book Discussions

Click on "Your Communities" from your basic Amazon profile page and search for communities dedicated to books in your niche. Jump into discussions and offer great advice. You can also find discussion groups from each product page. If a discussion group is dedicated to a book, it will appear on the book page. If not, start one!

Assignment #22—Listmania

Listmania is a list you can create, which contains links to similar books and products that you've found helpful. I've written lists on my top favorite vocal training books. People can view my lists on my product pages and on the pages of similar products. Amazon shoppers love lists, so let's help them out. It's time for you to create your own list. The link is on **amazon extras**.

Create at least one list on Listmania. When building your list, you'll be able to add details about the list. Create a cool name for your list like "25 ways to sing your brains out." Next, list your qualifications (author, singer), a description of your list, and tags that relate to your list. Add books and products to your list by clicking "Add product." Search for individual products, select the ones for your list, comment on the product, and then move on to the next item. Your goal is to add up to twenty-five books/products to your list.

Assignment #23—So You'd Like To . . .

"So you'd like to" pages are similar to Listmania lists but are more like an article or "guide" on a specific subject, such as, "So you'd like to learn about bass fishing." You write an article with good advice on a subject and suggest books (such as yours) in your guide that relate to the article. It's easy to add links to books/products by clicking on the "Insert a product link" button above the text body. Add your article by clicking on the link in **Amazon Extras.**

These tactics will help your book climb the rankings on Amazon, all for free. I think I should note here that just like other author scams, there are scams for the Amazon enthusiast as well. One such scam is the Amazon Best Selling Campaign. I received an email from a company stating they could make me a best-selling author on Amazon, and once I was an Amazon best-selling author, I'd be so for life, creating a frenzy of untold proportions for my books. I bought into the scheme for the sum of $2,800.

That gave me access to eight weekly teleseminars to master the company's method, which involved contacting companies and begging them to offer product discounts and freebies to people who bought my book through Amazon on one specific "book promotion" day. What took eight weeks could have been summed up in two hours.

Needless to say, I attempted the method and contacted companies that sold products that complemented my book. Once I convinced companies to give away freebies, I was required to beg and plead for them to send out a tailored email blast to their customer list on the chosen book-marketing blast day. The minimal number of emails sent out during the blast had to be approximately 1 million legitimate subscribers.

Herein lies the secret to the scam. Amazon updates book rankings every hour. If you were to jump to the No. 1 spot, that wouldn't mean you had sold millions of books. It would most likely mean that you'd sold between a few dozen and a few hundred books during that particular hour. Once you reached the No. 1 spot, you were supposed to take a snapshot of the screen and, *Ala Kazaam*, you were a best-selling author.

At the end of my campaign, I only reached position No. 1,870. Luckily, they offered a money-back guarantee but only refunded my money after I harassed them for weeks. Before refunding my money, the company stated that if I had reached a high ranking in a subcategory related to my book, such as "music: vocal instruction," I would have become a best-selling author in that category. That was never mentioned in their sales pitch. Regardless, I never reached a high-ranking position during that campaign in any category.

In the end, I received my refund with a note that said I was at fault for the failed campaign because my promotional ad copy for the Amazon book release (which was hosted on my website) had a black background with white ad copy and the reversal of standard color drove away buyers. Nonsense! It failed because there are too many factors involved, such as trusting participating companies to blast their email lists as well as not enough consumer interest on that specific day.

Even if I had spent sixty minutes at the No. 1 spot, it wouldn't have made me a best-selling author. It might have given me a fleeting sense of "best-selling author" fame, but after sixty-one minutes, I could kiss best-selling status goodbye. Take heed and steer clear of author-get-rich-quick schemes.

The only ones getting rich quick are the people charging $2,800 for the "training."

People now use Google to review books, and authors use it to increase book sales. The Google Book Search Partner program is similar to Amazon's Search Inside the Book. The author can choose to limit how much of their book can be viewed. A shopper can then order your print book or purchase access to an online version.

Is it wise to join Book Search? Well, with bit torrents at an all-time high because people believe it's not thievery, I think it's smarter to take the chance and at least try it out and let people review your entire book. If it's a good read, they'll buy it legally anyway. Find out how to join on the **book sales sites** *link.*

Don't underestimate the value of Barnes & Noble. It's still one of the biggest book chains in the world. Sign up, even if you don't shop through their site. Use it to participate in the B&N community, just as you would any other site. Help B&N sell more of your book by participating.

STEP SIX: BOOK SIGNINGS
One of the easiest ways to gain readers is book signings. Time for another assignment.

Assignment #24—Bookstore Contacts

Gather contact information for all local bookstores within a fifty-mile radius. You can browse your local phone book or Google "your area, your state: bookstores." Once you've added your information to the **bookstore contacts** list, move on to the next assignment.

Assignment #25—"Book" the Book Signing

This time, I want you to call the bookstore and ask to speak to the manager. Let the manager know who you are and what you've written. Offer to email your press kit and ebook, but also offer to meet face to face and present a physical copy of your book to leave with the manager.

Your goal is to set dates for your book signing at multiple stores. Once an agreement is made, you'll need to discuss legalities. Most likely the store will expect a percentage of every book sold. You must decide on the percentage. Depending on how the books are to be supplied, whether you bring them or they order a case from your distributor, the discount could be as high as 60%.

Assignment #26—Promoting Your Book Signing

You must promote your book signing, but also speak to the store manager to discuss what promotion they will do. Offer to supply marketing materials, such as posters, to the manager for marketing on your behalf.

Once you've established the bookstore's role in book promotion, focus on what you can do to promote the book signing. Remember all those local contact lists we crafted for newspapers and television stations? Begin emailing news releases to your contact lists announcing the date of your book signing. Let everyone know! Let your fans know on social networking sites, announce it on your Amazon author page, announce it on your website and through your blog!

Assignment #27—Announcement Sites

There are sites dedicated to author promotion that will allow you to announce your book signing. Check out the **book announcement sites** list and use the sites listed. Here are a few book-signing tips to make for a more enjoyable experience:

Posters. Create posters that feature a picture of you, your book, and a description of your book. They can be posted at the bookstore prior to your signing, and you can sell or give away autographed posters as well. You can have posters created through any of the sites on the **poster creation sites** list.

8X10 pictures. People love autographed mug shots. Photoshop your name on your image, save a jpeg to a jump drive, take it to any local store that has a photo department, and print several dozen copies. Sell them, give them away, or offer an autographed picture to everyone who buys your book. Bring a sharpie pen so that you can autograph them at the signing. People will appreciate the fact that you've personally autographed a picture for them.

Business cards. Order tailored business cards through one of the **business card design sites**. You always want a fan to have your contact information so they can join your mailing list, discover your next book, or contact you for other services.

Incorporate video. Another powerful tool for a book signing is video. If you've done any television shows or created a book trailer, bring a laptop or portable DVD player to play videos during your signing.

Colorful Book Stand. Have a book stand designed to hold your book. It adds flavor. Use a **book stand design** site.

Before proceeding to the next step, schedule at least one book signing.

STEP SEVEN: YOUR EMAIL LIST

You've been building email lists this entire chapter. Now it's time to expand it to include the emails of all your buyers and fans. Use your list for announcements, such as interviews, book signings, news about your next book, etc. Your subscribers will be happy to know that you have a new book or product coming soon, or an upcoming workshop.

Assignment #28—Cultivating Emails

Building an email list requires a system that allows your fans to sign up for the list through your site. If you're running your own site via a CMS platform, you'll find tools in your system to set up an automated mailing list. Personal mailing lists are worth their weight in gold because they're lists of people who are interested in your products. Remember, you can entice people to join your mailing list by offering something for free, such as an ebook, free report, or audio download. There are many **bulk emailing sites** that can automatically send automated email to your list, including attachments. I personally add the link where my subscribers can download their free report to the initial email they receive once they've joined my list.

Another way to collect emails is to save the email of everyone who buys your products through your website. I receive emails from my payment providers with each purchase, so I have the customer's contact info. I reply, thanking them for buying my book, and politely ask them to join my mailing list. This can be done automatically by customizing your thank-you email that's sent out via the shopping cart provider. A solid email list equals recurring income. Never pass up the opportunity to grow your mailing list.

STEP EIGHT: WRITE ARTICLES

Writing articles is one of the easiest ways to spread the word about you and your book. Articles can be a few paragraphs to a few pages long. The point is to share a bit of useful information, leaving the reader wanting more from you.

Assignment #29—Writing Multiple Articles

Create a new folder on your desktop for "Articles" and start writing today. Articles seed the Internet, enhancing your online presence. You can write on controversial topics, human interest, free tips, unusual events, unique products, editorial tie-ins, anything you can think of that leads them back to your book.

You can write articles on sections of your book. For instance, I could write articles about breathing tips, tips for sinus sufferers, ways to protect your voice in a crowd, teaching music online, etc. Think of at least ten article topics. Check jaimevendera.blogspot.com for my examples.

Once you have your list, begin writing the articles one by one. Add pictures, links, and videos if they enhance the article.

Check your articles for errors. Once an article is finished, save it in your folder.

Assignment #30—Submitting Articles
Submit three of your articles to the following **article listing sites**. Now that you've started submitting articles, adopt the habit of submitting at least one article per month to all the sites I've listed.

Assignment #31—Blogging
Add your articles to your blog. I'm assuming you have your blog listed on your website either on the homepage or on a BLOG link. If not, get it on there, pronto!

Tip: When you start interacting on several social networking platforms, it can become overwhelming trying to post your blogs to every single one of them. Refer to the **blog automation programs** list to simultaneously submit your latest blog to all your social networking sites.

STEP NINE: THE POWER OF VIDEO
Streaming video can skyrocket you to superstardom. For example, rock music icons Journey found their newest lead vocalist, Arnel Pineda, after watching him perform Journey songs on his YouTube channel.

By using video, you create a personal relationship with your audience, which can build your fan base. Time for another assignment.

Assignment #32—Making Videos
Videos are easier to create than you'd think. All you need is a video camera or a webcam, screen capturing software if you

plan to share something from your computer screen, and video-editing software.

For a webcam, refer to the **webcams** list for the best webcams available. There are many different types of **screen capturing software** on the market. And you'll need **video editing software**. I personally edit all my YouTube videos using Windows Movie Maker. In this assignment, we'll make three different types of video:

Video #1, Personal Video. Your personal video introduces you to your readers. It can be a two-minute message of you discussing your book while sitting at your computer, or it can be a ten-minute mini-movie of our "fishing" author talking to a video recorder while fishing. If you don't want to appear onscreen, use screen-capturing software to capture the screen while you open your ebook onscreen, flip through it, and explain a bit about your book and why you wrote it. They will see what you see on your screen.

Video #2, Demonstration Video. Create a video that covers a topic from your book. I've created videos on vocal health, hitting high notes, and how to scream, to name a few. This type of video gives your readers a taste of your expertise, leaving them wanting more.

Video #3, The Book Trailer. I had my own book trailer for my books on voice before I ever knew that book trailers existed. People are now making mini-movies based on their books that look just as good, if not better, than movie trailers. You can create your own book trailer using the resources from the **book trailer creation tools** list or you can hire someone through the

book trailer designers list. I've posted several **book trailer examples** that I've created.

Assignment #33—Posting Videos

Once you've filmed and edited your three videos, post them on your website, social networking sites, your Amazon author page, etc. Start several **video hosting** accounts. Read the guidelines for uploading your videos. Make sure to fill out the details for each video as you upload. Come up with an eye-catching name for each video, add a thorough description, and tag your video with keywords that will allow viewers to find you. Other important factors may include whether to allow voting, comments, etc. I usually allow all, but I only allow comments with approval.

STEP TEN: WEBINARS, WORKSHOPS, AND PRODUCTS

As a "how-to" writer, you should offer workshops, webinars, and private instruction to create multiple streams of income. Believe it or not, this is also a form of marketing, which is why I list it here. You can increase your fan base via workshops and increase your income by expanding your line to include more books as well as variations of your book such as workbooks, videos, audio programs, downloads, and other related products. I've conducted vocal workshops around the world and continue to create singing products based on my lessons and workshops.

If you can write a book, you can create a product line! Think beyond the book. If you wrote a fishing book, can you write a sequel to address another fishing problem? Can you write a book about boating that would tie in with fishing? Can you shoot a video of you demonstrating your fishing skills? Can you partner with a company and create your own set of lures?

Yes, you can!

Your goal isn't just to market your book; it's to market YOU with every workshop, webinar, and private consultation. I've gained loyal customers because of my workshops, so let's take a closer look.

WORKSHOPS

A workshop allows you to further explain the concepts in your book through in-person demonstration. For example, I created a mindset workshop dedicated to my Mindset book and techniques. I even created a free workbook to go along with the workshop.

Assignment #34—Creating a Workshop

Your book is your workshop. Open your book to page one and begin taking bullet points chapter by chapter in chronological order. Ask yourself, How can I teach the techniques in my book within a two-hour to four-hour workshop? (Your workshop can be longer, but I feel that two to four hours works best for most authors.)

Refine your bullet points as you visualize yourself physically demonstrating the techniques. Now you must think about how to pace the workshop and teach each segment in chunks. You must also allow for a few bathroom breaks and, above all, make it entertaining.

The key to making a workshop entertaining is audience participation. If I had to sit through a four-hour workshop just listening, I'd be snoring by the end of the first hour. Always include audience participation. Ask questions that the audience must answer, have participants fill out a workbook, let each person make their own fishing fly. Refer to one of the **workshop outlines** for examples on creating a workshop.

If a class runs short or long, don't panic. Make sure beforehand that the facility allows for an extra bit of time, in case you run long. If you run short, that's okay, too. People are not there to count minutes; they are there to learn.

If you need notes for a cheat sheet, use them; no one will care. Big-time speakers use keynotes. You can share your notes in a workbook or PowerPoint presentation. If you need more guidance for developing your workshop, check out the **workshop tools** list.

Assignment #35—Booking Workshops

Start local by contacting stores and venues for a place to host your workshop. Look in the phonebook or Google for stores in your area where you can teach. Add the contact info to the **workshop venues** list.

If I were doing a vocal workshop, I'd contact local music stores, schools, churches, and colleges for a facility. Use Google to find places that host workshops in your area. Simply Google "your area: workshop facilities" or "Your area: your subject: workshop or workshop facilities."

Make sure you understand financially what is required. Do you have to rent the facility? Will they allow you to use their facility for free? Will you have to share a percentage of registration fees and book sales? All this is important. Have a solid agreement first, and once the date is booked, begin marketing your workshop.

Assignment #36—Marketing Your Workshop

Use your contact lists to notify local news crews about your workshop. Now, get to work! I don't want to see you back here until you've conducted your first workshop!

Congratulations on creating your first workshop. How'd you do? WOW, you made that much? I guess I need to get back to conducting more workshops! For your next workshop, offer to pre-sale private instruction slots for after the workshop. Private instruction is a must, especially if you're conducting a workshop out of town, because a few private lessons can pay for your expenses.

If you're booking one-on-one consultations for after the workshop, you could request the facility to take pre-sales for private lessons for you. Depending on the number of pre-sales, you can either:

A. Start your workshop early, and conduct private sessions afterward.
B. Schedule two days in the area. Conduct the workshop on the first day, private sessions afterward and the next day.

The great thing about private consultations after a workshop is that it can lead to recurring income. If you're doing a local workshop, local students can continue to study with you on a regular basis. If it's an out-of-town workshop, you can offer virtual sessions via the Internet using one of the **video chat** sites. Let's move on to webinars.

Assignment #37—Conduct a Webinar

A webinar allows you to sit at your computer, conduct an online class, and make more money than a private consultation could earn. Let's say you offer one-on-one online lessons at $50 an hour. What if you could offer an "online workshop" for $20 per person and teach twenty people at a once? What if you double the time, and promote it as a $100 special for only $20?

What if you kick in a free workbook, to boost the value?

Let's look at what this means for your wallet. Twenty people attending your webinar or "online workshop" equals $400 for two hours' worth of work, $200 per hour, or four times the amount of your one-on-one hourly lesson price. You just quadrupled your hourly rate! Now, calculate what you could make if you conducted a webinar for a hundred people? Are you excited?

To host your webinar, you'll need a computer, a high-speed Internet connection, audio/visual capabilities such as a headset and webcam, and one of any of the current **virtual conferencing sites** for hosting the webinar. Once you're equipped, it's time to start promoting your first webinar.

Assignment #38—Promoting Your Webinar

Announce your webinar on every social networking site, blast your email list, and announce it on **webinar announcement sites**. You'll need to design a workbook based on your book for the class, but you already have one from your live workshop. You should promote the class at least two to three months in advance to build interest and take pre-sales, which you can do through your shopping cart and online payment processor. You simply create a new product through your shopping cart, limit the amount of participants, and then copy/paste the button code wherever you're promoting the class. It's easy and it's all explained through the help section of your shopping cart and payment processing sites. If it's overwhelming, pass it off to your webmaster if you have one.

Extra Credit

Your webinar is another product you can sell. You can capture the webinar with screen-capturing software. Most webinar service providers offer this option.

Assignment #39—Conducting More Webinars

Now that you've gotten your first webinar under your belt, you can book as many small, medium, or large webinars/classes per week, month, or year as you wish. Use the power of online conferencing to your advantage. ALWAYS design your webinars to do two things:

    A. Increase product sales
    B. Increase students

Always promote your books, products, and other services in every webinar. This brings us to our next assignment.

Assignment #40—Private Instruction

We've discussed private instruction for the last several pages. Private instruction can be done in person or via the Internet. Internet lessons require a computer, high-speed Internet connection, a virtual conferencing site, and audio/visual capabilities. If you're doing webinars, you're prepared for online lessons. Now you must let people know you're teaching. Check out my Kindle book, *Online Teaching Secrets Revealed* for more guidance.

Assignment #41—Announcing Your Teaching Business

Blast your list of subscribers and product purchasers, letting them know you're now accepting students. I also suggest adding a listing to your local phonebook.

How does someone book a lesson? They can schedule a lesson with you on the phone, or you can send them to the "book a session" page on your website. You need a page on your website that describes your teaching methods and explains

how to book live and online lessons. Check out www.
jaimevendera.com/lessons for reference.

You also need to create a way for someone to buy a time slot. You can create a "buy now" button within your payment platform or shopping cart. Once a person buys a lesson, you'll receive a confirmation. Then you'll have to email the person and schedule a time, or seek out an **automated calendars** option.

Assignment #42—Product Brainstorming

I've covered this topic, but I need to pound it into your head one more time before finishing this step. Begin brainstorming new products based around your book topic, including more books, mini-books, audio programs, video tutorials, etc. What if you videotaped your live workshops and offered the download as an additional product to your attendees? They buy it at the end of the workshop and provide you an email, and then you send them a digital download the next day. You now have their email address, which you can add to your list! What if you recorded your webinar and offered an instant download following the workshop? What if, as an additional feature, you offered to record a one-on-one session for the student at an additional 10%? You just created multiple video streams of income! You can create many products to sell on your website, after a workshop, and following webinars and online lessons.

STEP ELEVEN: CROSS-MARKETING

Cross-marketing is a way to spread your name among your community through websites and companies that are in your same field. Some companies sell advertising through their site, but our goal is to find companies in our field that would be interested in free cross-promotion. By supporting similar books, products, and companies, you give the consumer the information they seek. When people find sites linking to similar products, they'll be more likely to buy from both sites. We do this by link exchange.

Assignment #43—Link Exchange

A link exchange consists of each site posting a link or banner to the other site. You already have an arsenal of sites at your fingertips (if you've followed the SSBMS) that you can approach for link exchange, such as magazines that relate to your topic. Let's widen our horizons to include other sites similar to yours. It's time for more Google work. Go to Google and search for keywords based on your book subject. For a book about fishing, use keywords such as "fishing," "lures," "bass," "bluegill," "rod and reel," etc. Your goal is to find websites that are similar to yours and send them an email asking if they'd be interested in a link exchange.

Assignment #44—Affiliate Links

While adding link exchanges, check to see if the site offers an affiliate program. Sign up for affiliate programs to access your personal links and banner codes. When a person clicks through your affiliate link and buys a product, you earn a percentage commission.

If you have to list an actual affiliate link, here's a trick I use. I'll buy specific affiliate-like domain names and forward that domain name to my affiliate link. Affiliate links are always generic, like myaffiliate.com/jaime123xyz. By masking the affiliate link with a memorable website domain name, people can easily find you. If they like the affiliate product, more than likely they'll promote your domain name to friends. It's easier to remember a catchy domain name than a generic affiliate link. Some of my affiliate domain names include:

singerswater.com
vocal-flow.com
artistqlink.com

Join at least one new affiliate program during the link exchange assignment. Continue to add affiliate programs that suit your needs.

Create your own affiliate program, which will allow you to set the commission percentage, choose which items are listed as affiliate products, track each affiliate, and bulk pay each affiliate every month. Check out the **affiliate programs** *list. Join the affiliate club and spread your products around the world.*

I hope you've learned a lot during this chapter and have begun creating multiple streams of income along the way. Rinse, wash, and repeat the SSBMS once you've completed the first pass.

We've finally come to the end of *11 Simple Steps*. Once you've released your first book, I guarantee an idea for your second book is just around the corner. Pay close attention to your thoughts. Be ready to act on new ideas immediately. Continue to write and promote your book and begin conducting workshops, webinars, radio interviews, and book signings. After all, you are now an author, which means you are now considered an expert. Now prove it!